Rental Property Investing

How to invest in rental properties -

The keys to success

© Copyright 2018 by Calvin K. North - All rights reserved.

The follow eBook is reproduced below with the goal of providing information that is as accurate and reliable as possible. Regardless, purchasing this eBook can be seen as consent to the fact that both the publisher and the author of this book are in no way experts on the topics discussed within and that any recommendations or suggestions that are made herein are for entertainment purposes only. Professionals should be consulted as needed prior to undertaking any of the action endorsed herein.

This declaration is deemed fair and valid by both the American Bar Association and the Committee of Publishers Association and is legally binding throughout the United States.

Furthermore, the transmission, duplication or reproduction of any of the following work including specific information will be considered an illegal act irrespective of if it is done electronically or in print. This extends to creating a secondary or tertiary copy of the work or a recorded copy and is only allowed with express written consent from the Publisher. All additional right reserved.

The information in the following pages is broadly considered to be a truthful and accurate account of facts and as such any inattention, use or misuse of the information in question by the reader will render any resulting actions solely under their purview. There are no scenarios in which the publisher or the original author of this work can be in any fashion deemed liable for any hardship or damages that may befall them after undertaking information described herein.

Additionally, the information in the following pages is intended only for informational purposes and should thus be thought of as universal. As befitting its nature, it is presented without assurance regarding its prolonged validity or interim quality. Trademarks that are mentioned are done without written consent and can in no way be considered an endorsement from the trademark holder.

Table of Contents

Introduction 1

Chapter 1: Why Invest in Rental Property? 3

Chapter 2: Tips for Success 13

Chapter 3: Getting Started 21

Chapter 4: Analyze Potential Rentals 29

Chapter 5: Repair and Maintenance 39

Chapter 6: Rental Marketing Strategies to Try 47

Chapter 7: Tenant Types to Avoid 57

Conclusion 67

INTRODUCTION

Congratulations on downloading *Rental Property Investing: How to invest in rental properties - The keys to success* and thank you for doing so. When it comes to successfully making your first long-term investment, there are few better choices than real estate. After all, there's a reason that it is the oldest form of investing, bar none, largely due to its reliable returns and low barrier to entry.

Of the many types of real estate investment available, the best choice for new investors is typically rental property as, when orchestrated correctly, it allows the owner to offload most of the work of paying for the property to the tenants who will ultimately be living in it. There is more to the process than you might expect, however, which is why the following chapters will discuss everything you need to know to get your first investment property off the ground.

First, you will learn about the reasons why someone might want to invest in rental property to begin with, as well as the risks associated with doing so. Assuming you decide to press forward, you will then learn some key tips for success to keep in mind, before learning about what you need to do in order to get started on the right foot. Next you will learn how to analyze the properties you are looking at, as well as how to estimate renovations costs and ensure you can keep them as low as possible. From there you will learn how to ensure your property remains vacant for as short of time as possible with marketing strategies to try. Finally, you will learn about the types of tenants you are going to want to avoid, no matter what.

There are plenty of books on this subject on the market, thanks again for choosing this one! Every effort was made to ensure it is full of as much useful information as possible, please enjoy!

CHAPTER 1

WHY INVEST IN RENTAL PROPERTY?

When it comes to time tested investment options, it doesn't get much more reliable than real estate. As such, it is one of the core asset types that professionals recommend for any portfolio regardless if the holder is just starting out or simply looking to diversify. It offers a wide array of benefits when it comes to liquidity, profitability, cash flow, net worth and diversification which helps to ensure it is the right choice for a vast majority of investors.

Rental property overview

The most common type of real estate investment that most people are familiar with is purchasing a property with the goal of renting it out to a tenant who then pays a predetermined amount of rent for a set period of time. If you like the idea of having an investment that you can see, touch and even walk around in then it might be the type of investment for you.

In addition to turning a profit from the rental process itself, when you invest in a property you can expect to turn a profit in several other ways as well. First, you will profit from a concept known as appreciation. Appreciation happens naturally over time as the value of the property in the area around your holding increases in direct proportion to the level of scarcity the area is now experiencing when it comes to available property. You will also contribute to the appreciation of the property through any improvements that the local government makes to the area or that you make to the property itself. While it can certainly add up over time, you can typically expect about three percent per year, which means it should be thought of as a bonus to the other returns you see.

Depending on the type of real estate investment that you pursue, you may also be able to count on ancillary income via additional services that go along with your rental. For example, if you owned a small fourplex then you might also turn a profit by having laundry machines and vending machines on site. While this also likely won't amount to much on its own, when combined with appreciation it can be enough to offset repair costs, or just put a little extra in your pocket.

While these are both passive income streams you can count on for some investment properties, your active income stream for the property is going to come in the form of collecting rent on a tenant. When it comes to rental properties, assuming you charge a realistic amount for rent, and do your part to ensure a reliable residency rate, there is no reason you cannot expect to make a minimum of a seven percent return on your initial investment, every year, until the property is fully paid for at which point the returns would increase dramatically. A seven percent return on investment is about the same as what you can make investing in a reliable stock, or even for the first few years of owning a small business, and the risks are far lower.

While the risks associated with buying investment property are lower than many other types of investments, this doesn't mean that it still doesn't contain some element of risk. After all, the Great Recession proved that the housing market isn't bulletproof, despite what everyone thought at the time. This means that if you hope to get started investing in real estate, without the cash on hand to complete the transaction, then it is important to truly understand the value of the property in question, as well as the strength of the local, and national market, before you commit to anything.

If you find that an area is currently experiencing a period of price inflation then you are better off either looking somewhere else or go ahead with the deal only if you are fairly confident that a period of currency inflation is on its way which would mean the money you used to purchase the property would be worth more than that which was used to pay it back.

Types of rental properties

Rental properties tend to come in two main types, commercial and residential. Residential properties include things like vacation homes, apartment buildings, townhomes and multifamily and single-family homes. The average length of a lease in these situations is 12 months, with the specifics being left up to the landlord and the tenant. Commercial rentals are either warehouses, office buildings or retail space and the average lease is three years.

When it comes to deciding between the two types, commercial properties tend to be more passive overall, though they can be more difficult to fill initially, unless the area you are in is currently in the midst of economic uptick. On the other hand, as the length of the lease tends to be far longer, if you sign a lease at the wrong time, you could find yourself stuck with unfavorable rates for years to come.

Industrial rental space is the broadest category and spans everything from factory space to carwashes. Non-special use scenarios are similar to commercial real estate with one or more companies typically using the space over several years' time. Specific use locations, on the other hand, generate income from people paying to utilize the service over the length of the time you own the property.

Deciding if rental property investment is right for you

While financial planners recommend that everyone invest in real estate, and sooner than later if possible, that doesn't mean that doing so is automatically going to be the right choice for everyone, right now. In fact, there are several things you are going to need to consider before you make the leap, to ensure that the process is as smooth as possible. This means you are going to want to take a long hard look at your current situation and consider the following before you lock down and investing plans.

Consider the long-term: Current estimates put the amount that is required to retire at roughly $500,000 in the bank. Unfortunately for most American's they are saving less than $10,000 per year. If you are at a point in your life where you are stable enough to begin seriously considering investing, the first thing you are going to need to consider is your current level of income compared to your monthly bills.

Consider how you would pay for it: If you are currently saving money, but not taking the extra step to maximize your returns, then odds are you will be able to do more with you already have. This is why saving and investing are two separate things. Saving is a passive active, investing, even if you are doing so in a passive income stream is still considered a passive act.

Furthermore, you are going to need to keep in mind that, despite the fact that there are numerous different ways of generating the capital to purchase your first rental property, very few of them don't require a significant down payment upfront. Furthermore, it is important to keep in mind what your current level of financial stability, along with your credit score, to ensure you will be able to easily get a loan for the amount you are looking for.

If you don't feel as though your finances are where they need to be, this doesn't mean that investing in real estate is beyond you at the moment. Rather, it means you will just need to work harder to reach the same goals. Alternately, you will need to be more willing to take on investments of a speculative nature, and rely on luck, at least for your first real estate purchase.

Consider your contingency plan: It is important to keep in mind that investing in real estate for rental purposes is also going to require having a backup plan assuming things don't work out as you hoped. This frequently manifests itself in the form of unexpected required repairs which means that if you are going to be able to pay for the property, but not afford and extra 20 or 30 thousand dollars for unexpected repairs, you may need to hold off to avoid ending up in a situation where you can't afford to stick with the property and you can't afford to sell either.

Consider your support system: While having a support system is always recommended when it comes to making the wisest investments possible, it is especially crucial when you are first getting into real estate investment as there are so many different variables that need to be accounted for in order for the investment to turn out the way you are anticipating. Knowing that you have someone available to run potential deals by can make it easier to invest with confidence so you don't have to worry about secretly losing your shirt with your first deal.

Real estate investment is far more complex than simply purchasing a property and then finding someone else to live in it which means you will likely benefit greatly from the knowledge that other local real estate investors could provide. The best place to find others like you is through a real estate investment club. These clubs operate in many cities and towns across the country, and can provide you with a wealth of key information about your area you won't find anywhere else.

CHAPTER 2

TIPS FOR SUCCESS

As a new investor in the real estate market, you will likely find that every move you consider making fills you with anxiety, simply each and every action has the potential to affect you so greatly for good or for ill. This is a natural part of the learning process, however, and learning while doing is naturally going to lead to some mistakes now and then. Keeping the following tips in mind will ensure you keep those mistakes to a minimum and avoid common new investor pitfalls in the process.

Avoid viewing a property without a plan: For the best results, you are never going to want to get to the part of the process where you actually view a property without first having a clear idea of just how you would use the property if your offer was accepted. What's more, you should have already done your own research on the property as otherwise it will be difficult for you to make a bid that is both fair and reasonable, while at the same time allowing you the room you need to make a profit when you rent it out. When it comes to ensuring your first investment property works out as planned, you likely won't have much wiggle room to work with which means that keeping a close eye on your numbers is key if you hope to stay on track.

It is common for many new investors to find themselves in a scenario where they see a property that they feel is too good of a deal to pass up, ignoring the fact they don't actually know anything about the price of property in the area. When considering a potential investment, it is important to keep in mind that just because a specific property is a good deal, doesn't mean it is the right deal for you, right now. With your first real estate investment you likely have too much on the line to do yourself the disservice of moving forward with a given property until you known you have a course of action that is airtight and ready to go.

Keep your expectations in check: While it is always possible to find a turnkey property for under market value that you can scoop up and start making a profit on immediately, this is without a doubt the exception, not the rule. Depending on the amount you are able to get for a loan, you may need to start with a property that needs some work, or you may be able to get a property that is ready to go, but you will have to pay at or near the asking price to get it.

Depending on your personal circumstances, you will need to determine a realistic timeframe when it comes to just how long everything is going to take, and also how long you can expect before you start turning a profit. Dotting your Is and crossing your Ts beforehand will ensure that you embark on your new investment opportunity with a clear understanding of the financial and mental tribulations to come. To understand the timeframe you are likely looking at, consider just what all a successful investment entails.

First you will need to do the research on the area you are considering investing in as well as researching numerous different options before finding one that meets your needs. Then, once you make an offer, you can expect to wait for upwards of three months if you have gone ahead and gotten preapproval through a traditional bank. Even if everything is aces, you will still likely need to factor in about a month before your name is on the deed.

From there, you will need to consider any improvements that you are going to make to the property, as well as any repairs that need to be completed before you can start looking for renters. Generally speaking, you can expect a residential property to sit empty for between one and three months, assuming it is not located in a high demand area before you find the right tenant. Speed is not one of real estate's investing's virtues but what it lacks in quick turnaround times it makes up for in reliability.

Trying to do it all by yourself: While having faith in yourself is an admirable quality, when it comes to real estate investment odds are not only will you not be able to do it all yourself, you are almost certainly not going to want to. While some people will have all the skills required to complete a house full of renovations all by themselves, the time that this will take will almost always mean that this is a poor value proposition at best. Likewise, while you could provide all the services your future tenants could need, finding a property management company to do this work for you can turn your investment into a true passive income opportunity.

Real estate investment is a numbers game which means that you will always see greater overall returns by taking a smaller personal cut of each property and working quickly and efficiently with a team than trying to make as much profit as possible and doing it all yourself. At the very least, you are going to need a real estate investment lawyer, a CPA and a reliable contractor.

Once you have built up key relationships, the importance of keeping them going cannot be overstated. These relationships will often be the difference between failure and success as you will be working with these people regularly to ensure your passive income stream keeps operating smoothly. This means you are going to want to go beyond the traditional customer/service person relationship and form bonds that extend both ways and ensure they will keep your best interests in mind when it comes to it. While this extra effort will likely seem superfluous at first, if you keep it up you will find this practice pays serious dividends in the long-term.

Always strive for the best price every time: While you won't be able to get your target price for every property you purchase for investment purposes, this doesn't mean you should be too eager to negotiate to close the deal either. While the occasional concession to close a deal is fine, doing it too often can end up seriously hurting your bottom line on a new potential rental property, easily making it difficult, if not impossible to turn a profit using your original plan.

As such, when going into any negotiation you are going to want to keep in mind what your ideal purchase price for the property as well as the maximum number you can go to and the number that you are going to have to walk away from as it will only cause you to take a loss. What's more, it is important to never get so caught up in walking away with a property that you ignore these numbers as doing so is only going to cause you additional problems when it comes to ensuring your numbers actually line up.

Furthermore, you are going to want to apply these principles to everything you purchase for the property, regardless if it costs $1 or $100,000. While smaller items might not seem worth the hassle of finding the best price, these incidentals can add up over time, leading to a loss on what could have very well been a profitable venture. Avoid a lax attitude and always be away of the true costs of any concessions you make to ensure you are still on track for your bottom line.

Never sign anything without reading it: After going through all of the trouble of doing their research on a particular property, coming up with a plan and doing their best to stick with it through the offer phase, many new real estate investors then get so eager to seal the deal that they sign whatever is placed in front of them without reading it thoroughly. Not taking the time to understand the finer points of a contract you sign, either to purchase the property or to agree to the loan, is akin to gambling with your long-term investment, a poor choice regardless of the specifics. Not taking the time to understand your contract can easily cause you to end up paying thousands more than you anticipated, based on incorrect expectations, a costly and easily preventable mistake.

Get serious: Just because a real estate investment is unlikely to pay off in the short-term is no reason to approach it with a casual manner, especially if you hope to make a profit in the long run. Your real estate investments are a business whether you think of them that way or not, and if you ever hope to see the results of your hard work you need to show real dedication and commitment to the idea from start to finish. Remember, when it comes to investments you will only ever get back from them what you put in multiplied by the amount of effort you put forth.

CHAPTER 3

GETTING STARTED

Before you can hope to start purchasing property successfully, it is crucial that you have a solid investment plan in place. Building a personalized investment plan will help to ensure you are actively working towards specific goals as opposed to simply investing randomly and hoping for the best. Don't forget, if you aren't already on track to save $500,000 by the time that you retire then you are not saving enough to support yourself through retirement. If your long-term investment potential could use some help, try the following steps to point you in the direction of a plan that works for you.

Start with the big picture: The first thing you are going to need to determine when it comes to creating a personalized real estate investment plan is the reasons behind why you want to invest and the amount of time you are comfortable before you start seeing returns. This doesn't mean you need to have a clear plan outlined in your head at this early point, but you will find that having a general outline will make it easier to determine the steps you need to take moving forward.

Consider primary objectives: When you start putting your plan together, you are going to need to consider what your short-term goals are, probably research, as well as what your long-term objectives for your investments as well. Generally speaking these objectives can be classified in one of three ways, either as relating to income, safety or growth.

If your primary goal is the safety of your investment then you are going to want to ensure that the investment you choose has the lowest level of risk possible. If, instead, you are interested in generating a steady stream of long term income then you will be looking to balance out risk and reward and if you are interested in growth then you will be mostly focused on the long term.

Understand your affinity for risk: When it comes to investing successfully, the first thing you need to understand is that without risk, there is no reward. For example, a turnkey property is far less of a risk than a property that needs some work before you can rent it out, which is why the price is going to be much higher on the first than it is the second.

Essentially, if you are more prone you are towards making investments that might not pay off, but when they do they pay off big, then you are going to have a higher general tolerance for risk than someone that is prone to always taking the sure thing in any situation. When discussing risk, properties that are going to generate a higher rate of return in exchange for being less of a sure thing are considered volatile and reliable investments are considered non-volatile.

When it comes to investing in real estate successfully, the greater the amount of speculation required at the point of commitment, the greater the amount of volatility that investment is said to have. While a property that requires a lot of work can definitely generate a larger return in the end, the fact that you need to accurately predict a far greater number of things off the bat means you will likely want to pick a simpler project for your first real estate investment. If you prefer low volatility strategy, then you are going to be able to get by with fewer overall quality investments while a high volatility strategy will involve many more investments overall due to the fact that you have to account for failed risky investments as well.

Consider your emotions: While knowing the numbers is a big part of successfully starting down the path of real estate investment, there is still more to consider as well. When it comes to making a successful plan, you also need to know how likely you are to let your emotions run wild when you are in the thick of it. This means taking a realistic look at yourself and understanding how likely you are to do things like throw your plan aside in favor of a gut feeling at the last minute or pay more than you should for a property because you don't like to lose.

If you are unsure how you would act when money was on the line and you were considering a potential property, you may want to try the following exercise. Start by picturing a pair of intersecting lines. The line that is horizontal can be thought of as the difference between those who are confident and those who are anxious. The vertical line can then be thought of as the difference between those who are careful and those who are impetuous. Gauge yourself on these two lines and then pick the quadrant that you would most likely fall into. If you can't choose then you likely have equal amounts of all the qualities.

Figure out how you will be paying for it

Look into lenders: You will likely find that you are able to stick with a plan you have prepared ahead of time more easily if you are already preapproved for a loan for a set amount. This will allow you to work a firm price into your plan that you can realistically afford, taking out much of the remaining potential guess work in the process.

When approaching a traditional lender, you are going to want to ensure you have at least 20 percent of your target amount on hand and ready to put down when you find the right property. If you plan on looking outside the box for a lender then you are going to want to instead have as much on hand as possible as it will only improve your chances.

Additionally, you will want to take the time to look at different lenders in your area, and really go out of your way to choose the one that you like the most as the more you work with the same individual the better your rates will ultimately be. Every lender is going to have different rates and policies, so you will find that it is really beneficial to look around before making your final choice.

If you instead take the time to forsake the more traditional lenders in favor a more local option, you will likely lose out on some frills, but will ultimately end up with a more personalized approach overall as well as a lender that is more likely to be willing to work with a new investor with less than perfect credit. Rather than being just another account, you can trust that you are building a long-term relationship that includes a strategy that works for everyone.

When it comes to considering various local lenders, it is important that you keep in mind the number of investors they are working with, along with the amount of capital the firm has available to lend, as well as the types of real estate it most frequently deals in. Most importantly, however, you will want to consider the number of loans you will be able to take out at one time, though only if you are planning on making buying rental properties a habit. Starting with these questions will make it easier for you to find a lender who matches your personality, as well as your skill set and bank account while also ensuring that you don't waste your time or the time of the lenders you didn't choose.

When approaching a lender, you will want to do so with a well thought out and researched plan that shows a high value to loan ratio as well as a credit score of 740 or higher if you hope to score the best interest rates. If your credit score is lower, the only way you can expect the same rate is by paying more or by paying the same amount and taking a higher interest rate. Regardless, you will want to be able to show that you have the ability to pay all of your expenses for a full six months, plus the expenses of the new property as well if you hope to be considered acceptable.

Generally speaking, as a new investor you are typically going to have better luck when it comes to approaching local banks as they will have more of a vested interest in keeping the local economy as flush as possible. They will also often have options that are far more flexible and even potentially especially tailored for investors who are starting out along with brokers who have directives to finance those who are just starting out. Even still, it is important to not simply take the first rate that is offered you, without doing your research first. If you are already working with a local real estate investment club then they are the best place to start when it comes to getting lender recommendations.

CHAPTER 4

ANALYZE POTENTIAL RENTALS

As a new real estate investor, it can be easy to get too caught up in the hunt for a good price and move forward without thinking everything through. This is a recipe for disaster, however, which means you will want to avoid this compulsion whenever possible. Instead, you are going to want to keep the following considerations in mind in order to ensure you end up with the right real estate investment for you that generates a regular profit for years to come.

Choosing the right type of property

When it comes to choosing the best future rental property for you, the first type of property you should consider is the condominium as they make a great choice for the first-time rental property investor for several reasons. First of all, you are more likely to attract young professionals with this type of property which means you can count on things such as receiving the rent on time and minimal damage to the property that will need to be repaired between tenants. When purchasing a condo you will also be purchasing an onsite property management company along with a strict housing association that handles all of the daily work. The downside to condos is that the rents tend to be lower as does the rate of appreciation.

Alternately, you may want to consider single family homes as renters in these properties are both typically willing to pay more than those who rent condos, and also often plan on staying for more than year which means you can easily build a long-term relationship with them. Furthermore, these properties are also far more likely to contain multiple individuals with jobs, which means it is less likely that they will miss a monthly payment. These individuals are more likely to have higher demands on the property and you as a landlord, however, so this should be taken into account as well.

Finally, a small apartment building or duplex allows you the guaranteed stability of multiple individuals or families which means statistically most of them will always be full or pay their rent on time. Property management companies are also more likely to takes these types of jobs from new landlords, which is great if you are looking for a largely passive income stream. The individual rents will likely be much lower in these situations, however, and you will need to initially worry about finding renters to fill all of the spaces if they are currently empty.

When you decide on the type of property that seems right for you, you will want to consider options that appear to promise the greatest overall projected appreciation rates, as well as those with a reliable projected cash flow. Don't forget to factor in the possibilities of vacancies as well. When it comes to looking at listings, you are going to want to look at those within your price range, as well as those just above as there is a possibility those prices could drop. Ideally you will be looking for properties that can be spruced up with just some minor changes between renters to keep it feeling fresh and modern. At this point it isn't as important to focus on what the property looks like in the moment as it is to focus on the long-term potential.

After you have found a property that appears as though it fits your qualifications, you are then going to want to hire a professional to come out and ensure that things like the foundation and major systems are all up to par. This includes the roofing, electrical and plumbing systems. Once you know just what is going to need to be repaired, you can determine a fair price for the property that benefits both sides.

Consider the overall floorplan: While a two bedroom one bath might sit on the market for months in some areas, renters would likely be beating down the door if it was a three bedroom instead. Specifics like this are the reason that once you are inside the property you are going to want to consider the overall floorplan instead of how things are currently arranged. Obviously, you will want to avoid the type of work that results in moving load bearing walls, but anything that is inessential can be taken down for a very reasonable cost. You will want to consider the current trend when it comes to the flow of things but it is important that you don't let current space configurations stop you from seeing what the potential is instead.

Get the lay of the land

In addition to finding out the details of the property itself, you are also going to want to ensure that you get the lay of the land to ensure you understand exactly what it is that you are getting yourself into.

Consider the neighborhood: First things first, you are going to ensure that when you are driving through the neighborhood your potential rental property is in, you keep your eyes peeled. The specifics of the neighborhood will make it easier for you to get a feel for the type of renter who would be comfortable calling the place home, which can make it easier for you to get an idea of the type of floorplans and amenities you are looking for.

Furthermore, this trip will make it possible for you to get a better feel for the neighborhood as a whole, which means you are going to want to speak to current residents, ideally renters if you can manage it as they will have no qualms about sharing the neighborhoods dirty laundry. While negative opinions at this stage can be disheartening, it is important to not immediately consider them to be deal breakers, after all, they could be used as bargaining chips if the price is right.

Consider the tax rate: As real estate investing is a long-term investment, it is important that you consider the local tax rate so you can make an informed decision about the properties you are considering. Remember, the rate that is charge can vary dramatically from neighborhood to neighborhood, so it is always best to double check the local rates to ensure you are not in for a nasty surprise down the road. Sometimes a higher tax rate comes along with a noticeably nicer area, other times it can change seemingly at random, regardless, forewarned is forearmed.

Dig deeper: In addition to looking into an area to see what you can see, you are also going to want to dig a little deeper in order to get a true feel for the neighborhood. This should start with an evening drive-through, to start, but you will also need to look into the local crime rate which can be done by simply taking a trip to the local police station. There you will find everything you could need when it comes to rates for petty crime, vandalism, as well as more serious crimes as well. You will also want to ask around and see how much time officers spend in the neighborhood as driving past police cars on the way to your property is hardly the way you will want to introduce potential renters to it. Finally, you are going to want to do an online search for the neighborhood as well, you never know what you might find.

Look into what plans the city might have for the area: When you are looking into a specific area, you are also going to want to take time to consider what plans, if any, the city has in the works. In fact, keeping an eye on local city council meetings is a great way to ensure that you are up to date on everything that city is planning, so you can put it to use down the line. Doing so could help you to buy in early into a neighborhood that is getting a major new amenity, or it could save you from having to deal with years of construction making it difficult to rent out your property. This type of information is readily available on a local government website, yet it is often overlooked by new real estate investors, don't make their mistake, do your homework.

See what else is around: While a few for rent signs can be expected in any neighborhood, a higher number than average could mean one of several things, none of which are particularly good for you. First, it could mean the property is seasonal, such as a college town, which can work to your advantage if you are willing to accept seasonal vacancies. If you can work within the confines of the seasonal system you can likely ensure that these properties are easily filled during the busy season, and for a premium besides.

It could also simply mean there is lots of competition in the area, which means you are better off looking somewhere else unless the supply does not appear to meet the demand. Finally, it could mean that there is something wrong with the area that is causing lots of homeowners to look for other uses for their homes than living in them, which is hardly encouraging. Regardless, it is important that you do your homework before making any snap purchasing judgements in these types of areas.

CHAPTER 5

REPAIR AND MAINTENANCE

Ideally, you will be able to find a property that is in relatively good condition for a price that works within the bounds of what you have been preapproved for. At this point, many new real estate investors make the mistake of trying to spruce up their new property to the levels they would expect when looking at a house to buy, not to rent. Renters are not buyers, however, which means they are often willing to accept far less when it comes to overall quality.

This doesn't mean you can leave an interior dingy, or dangerous, but it does mean you don't need to worry about the long-term health of any of the major systems or smaller, finishing touches. Additionally, things like the presence or absence of fans, light fixtures or the color of the paint on the walls are all acceptable as long as they work, and or remain largely neutral. What could easily be a sticking point with buyers will typically pass by renters without a word.

Instead, when it comes to considering what needs to be done, you should think of everything in terms of overall cost, not just in the short-term but in the long-term as well. As such, while you may not want to replace any major systems before your first tenant, it is important to think about the fact that it is far easier, and cheaper to fix an air conditioner or furnace when you have the time to shop around for prices, something that's not really an option when tenants are breathing down your neck.

Making improvements on the cheap

When it comes to ensuring that your renovations are going to proceed both smoothly, and under budget, keep the following tips in mind to ensure you keep costs down without sacrificing tenant happiness in the bargain.

Break things down to their core components: While thinking about everything that needs to be done to get a property tenant ready, even if the property is in fairly good shape, can be enough to make you start hyperventilating; you will find that things proceed far more smoothly if you first take the time to break them down to their core components. Not only will this make it easier to cope with everything that needs to be accomplished, it will help you save money because you will be able to determine all of the required purchases up front, allowing for a greater chance of getting a discount on bulk. You are going to want to go room by room and make a list of everything that needs to be done so then you can easily go back through the list prior to listing the property so that you can ensure everything was done according to plan.

Cut costs in the right places: While you will definitely want to ensure that you sand off all of the rough edges on your new property, as a general rule of thumb you can shy away from any improvements that you don't believe will either make the property easier to rent out, or cause the amount you can collect in rent to increase. First things first, this means you are going to want to renovate the bathrooms and the kitchen.

Updating these two rooms can improve the overall feel of a home that is teetering on the edge and you can often get by with improvements to just these two rooms alone. Even better, you can often get by with just switching out the cabinet doors, the fixtures and the countertops. If you are looking to go for the absolute budget options, you can adequate refit two rooms for around $1,000.

Stick with neutral colors: When it comes to making changes to the color scheme of a property, it is important to always choose neutral colors that will work with as many different color pallets as possible, excluding plain white. Doing so will ensure that it is as easy for potential renters to picture themselves in the space as possible. What's more, you can often find plenty of neutral paint colors in the bargain bin of your local paint store, ensuring you can pick them up for pennies on the dollar. Alternatively, you may find it easier to buy neutral paint colors in bulk when they are on sale so that you know you will be ready to repaint between renters for years to come.

Bargain shopping isn't just buying cheap: When it comes to getting your initial investment property renter ready, it can be tempting to use the cheapest possible parts and products to save money prior to starting to see the property pay dividends. It is important to avoid this impulse, however, as you will typically find that cheap products wear out nearly twice as fast as quality products, while only saving you about a third of the price ensuring they end up actually costing you more in the long run. Remember, finding a middle ground between cost and quality is often the better choice, simply to avoid having to spend the additional costs in labor a second time.

Consider your suppliers carefully: When it comes to sourcing the materials for your first investment property, it is important to take the extra time to do some exploratory legwork early on to ensure you know you are getting the best prices throughout the process. It is also important that you have a list that accounts for absolutely everything you need as running to the store to buy a spare part here and there is one of the biggest drains on the profits that new real estate investors see on their first projects as they forget to factor in these types of costs early on.

Purchasing your products in bulk from a local supplier will not only allow you to price things out more accurately ahead of time, but it can provide you with an avenue for potential significant savings as well. To see these savings in action all you are going to need to do is simply seek out your local hardware options before asking to speak with a manager.

Once you have the right person's attention, all you need to do is go over your list of required items with them before explaining that this is your long term investment strategy and that you will likely be buying these items in bulk several times a year. With a clear idea of just what it is you are offering, all you need to do is to then ask if there is anything the manager can do for you in exchange for assurances that you will be purchasing all of your required items at their store. While this won't work with every manager at every store, it shouldn't take more than a few tries before you find someone who is willing to make a deal.

Always be on the lookout for a great deal: A great way to ensure that you never have to stoop to paying full price for the kinds of items you are sure to always need more of, is always keep an eye out for sales regarding these items. Then, you can simply buy in bulk when the savings are high, confident you will ultimately need whatever it is at some point later on. On the other hand, if you find that you are always running out of this or that, you may find it useful to buy in bulk early on, just to save yourself the hassle later on.

One great example of this is the granite that is a quick and easy way to improve the feel of any bathroom. Luckily, as much of the granite in a bathroom sink is going to be removed anyway, you can often find great deals on flawed granite that is only going to be removed later on. With a bit of practice, you will be hard pressed to ever pay more than pennies on the dollar for your smaller granite countertops.

Always consider the cost benefit analysis: When it comes to determining if a given renovation option is actually worth your time, you are going to want to take both the short and long-term costs of completing the project versus letting it be. Often you will find options that are sure to work for a round of renters, maybe two, but eventually quick fixes will need to be dealt with in a more permanent fashion. When it comes to determining if a quick job makes more sense than a complicated one, consider what it will cost to do the quick job two or three times before making any decisions.

Likewise, if you amortize the costs of doing a job right the first time, out over several years you will often find that the costs of doing the job properly end up being cheaper overall, which won't do much to ease the initial sting, but will help your overall bottom line. Don't forget, a rental real estate property is a long-term investment, be sure to treat it as such.

CHAPTER 6

RENTAL MARKETING STRATEGIES TO TRY

In the end, it doesn't matter what work you've done to get to this point, eventually all of your hard work is going to come down to your ability to successfully market your property to the potential tenants out there. This means that you are going to want to do everything in your power in order to ensure that it is not only marketed as widely as possible, but also that the marketing targets the right audience. Don't forget, each day that your property sits vacant is a day that you are losing money so the sooner you find a tenant the better off you'll be.

Get the word out: When it comes to ensuring as many people see your listing as possible, the first thing you are going to wan to do is to post it on as many different property listing sites as possible. The major names in this space these days include Craigslist and Zillow, but you will also want to look into any local options. Local choices are always going to be preferable as they are going to find a far more targeted audience ready and willing to move into your property sooner rather than later.

When you do post to these sites, it is important that you do so in the correct way to ensure that the return on your time and effort is going to be worth it. This means you are going to want to spend some time before you start writing up your ad brainstorming the strengths of the property in question as well as relevant details and a catchy title that will stand out amongst all the simply descriptive titles that potential renters are more likely to brush past without clicking on and exploring further. If you are having a difficult time coming up with things to write about, you may find it helpful to reflect on the reason that you purchased the property in question and then use that fact as the basis of your sales pitch.

When putting together your ad, you are going to want to do everything in your power to portray the property in the best way you can, without going so far as to hype expectations above what the property can deliver on. Nothing is worse for a potential tenant's enthusiasm than unmet expectations right from the jump. Again, this is not to say that you shouldn't talk up your property's better qualities, it is just to reiterate that honesty really is the best policy. Furthermore, when writing your ad it is important that you don't wax so poetic that you leave out key details like square footage, number of bedrooms and bathrooms, pet and smoking policy and the like.

These days it is also important to include as many high-quality photographs of the property as possible. Even better, you are going to want to arrange them so that, when viewed, they accurately simulate a walkthrough of the property. These photos are extremely important to the effectiveness of your ad and should be treated as such. What this means is that if you are bad at taking pictures, it is more than worth your while to find someone else to take them for you. Whatever the cost, you will certainly recoup it with the added spice the right pictures will add to your listing.

Finally, before you sit down to write, take the time to make a list of all of the things that really set the property apart from other rentals in the area. Potential renters always like to hear about renovated kitchens and bathrooms, but any major changes to other rooms are always welcome as well. Likewise, be sure to mention extra-large backyards, RV gates, extra large garages and anything that sells to a target audience all deserve a mention.

Don't forget social media: One of the only good parts about social media is the fact that it lets people from around the world form friendships that transcend space and last a lifetime. Those with the motivation to do so, like you, can then exploit those relationships for personal gain. Specifically, thanks to social media it is statistically likely everyone on your friends list either knows someone who is planning a move or knows someone who knows someone who is getting ready to move. As such, posting the details of your listing on social media, and bugging your friends and family to share the posting as well, is a great way to practically guarantee that someone interested is going to see it.

Currently, an estimated 40 percent of those who are under the age of 30 found their current residence via social media which means this is an extremely valuable tool assuming you choose to monetize it correctly. While you will certainly want to post your new investment on your personal feed, if you plan on regularly purchasing new rental properties then you might instead find it more useful to go ahead and create a social media presence for your rental real estate investment business as it will certainly come in handy every time you have a vacancy that you are going to need to have filled as quickly as possible.

Doing so will make it easy for you to have a dedicated space to filling any vacancies that you need filled, though you will need to do far more than just repost your listings if you hope to be successful. Instead, you will need to create a page that is devoted to the area that your property is located in, either to the neighborhood or something even more specific depending on the number of residents in question. You should choose a region that is large enough to warrant interest from locals, while still being small enough to instill local pride.

This strategy is effective as oftentimes locals are legitimately interested in the comings and goings of their neighborhood, but there is nobody to take charge and curate the space, gather all of the relevant information and post it in a place that is easily accessible. If you take the time to do the leg work and collect this information for people, you will be providing a useful service, that will pay dividends when it comes to filling vacancies as quickly as possible.

Beyond posting details about local events, you will also want to include things like local news stories along with other types of local content that you believe will get people to start actively engaging with your page, and with one another. You may also want to include polls, even prizes, anything to ensure your potential tenants keep checking back on the page time and again. What's more, having such a thriving community page will ensure the page shows up on the Google search results for people doing research on the area, enticing other people to live in such an active community.

When you do post content advertising your rentals, a good rule of thumb is to ensure that it doesn't make up more than 10 percent of all of your posts on the page, which should include several new items per day. If you lay the groundwork and get people in the neighborhood talking about your page, then your name and the community are going to be linked which is the best type of marketing a landlord could ask for.

When it comes to truly maximizing your social media effectiveness, it is crucial that you think of every post, no matter how minor, in terms of its potential for free advertising, and treat it with the appropriate level of importance. Social media can be an immensely powerful tool when it comes to ensuring you are not only able to keep your rental properties full, but actually have a waiting list so when a new property opens up you have a new tenant ready and waiting without skipping a beat.

Open house: While you will want to start off by making it very clear you are renting the property out as opposed to selling, holding an open house is a perfectly acceptable way to get the word out about your property, especially if you really put in some extra work to spruce things up in the interim. One of the key elements to be effective in this scenario is to have a very clear idea of how much the renovations to the property cost before you purchased it, as well as pictures of the before portion of the process whenever possible. There is nothing more effective when it comes to ensuring that a property looks as good as possible than pictures of what it used to look like before. Pictures plus a list of what has been accomplished will go a long way towards making the rental price for the property seem perfectly reasonable.

During the event you will want to do everything in your power to ensure the property is at its absolute best and also do what you can to sweeten the deal. This could mean sacrificing some amount of profits in order to ensure the property remains vacant for the shortest period of time possible. Good examples of this are promising to pay the utilities for a few months, offering an introductory rental price or even cutting down on the required deposit for qualified tenants.

CHAPTER 7

TENANT TYPES TO AVOID

In a perfect world, you, as the landlord, could expect to provide a quality service and, in turn, be treated with respect by a tenant who is eager to make the process as simple for everyone involved as possible. This is rarely the case, however, and if you aren't careful you can find yourself dealing with a tenant that costs you time as well as money. While you will eventually develop a quality screening process that works for you, for now you will likely find it helpful to keep an eye out for the following types of tenants, so you can avoid them at all costs.

The destructive tenant: There is no type of tenant worse for your newly minted rental property than the destructive tenant. Whether they have a destructive child or pet that they have no control over, remodel a portion of the property to better suit their needs, or are simply not respectful to the property, this type of tenant is likely to cause extreme damage to your property and then try and do their best to get you to pay for it.

Luckily, it is often possible to pick out a destructive tenant when they come to look at the property, as long as you think to look for the signs. First, you are going to want to be sure to meet them by their vehicle as its condition will often give you a good idea of what you can expect when your property is under their care. If they have children, then you will want to pay attention to how well-behaved they are. The children don't need to be perfect, they are children after all, but there is a big difference between a normal child and one that is willfully destructive. Regardless of how they present themselves during the walkthrough, you will always want to call the previous landlord and ask about the state of the property when the tenant moved out.

The loud tenant: Noisy tenants can be some of the most frustrating of all, regardless of whether or not you live near enough to hear the ruckus yourself. This is because, as the landlord, the other tenants or neighbors will (rightly) direct their complaints at you if the issue doesn't resolve itself in a timely fashion. This can be made all the worse by the fact that otherwise, a loud tenant might by ideal, respectful to the property and liable to always pay their rent on time. Nevertheless, when you start getting daily calls about the noise, you will start to wish you had never allowed them to sign the lease.

While it can be easy to pick out likely signs of potential loud tenants, questions about parties, surround sound hookups, stories about rowdy friends, none of these are reason enough to disqualify a given tenant. As such, you need to do your best to make it clear what the general neighborhood atmosphere is like in your ad, in hopes of naturally attracting likeminded individuals. Keep in mind, if an applicant turns in an application, you are legally required to respond and tell them why they did not qualify for the property, which means you may need to be on the lookout for a valid reason if you feel the biggest disqualifying factor is noise.

The deadbeat tenant: Generally speaking, as a landlord you should be able to handle anything short of a destructive tenant, assuming they pay their rent on time. Unfortunately, the deadbeat tenant is going to be able to come up with just about every trick in the book to avoid doing just that. What's worse, as this is rarely the first time they have found themselves in this position, they are likely experts on just what they can get away with which means you should be prepared for them to owe hundreds, at least, in back rent at any given time.

Luckily, as this is rarely their first rodeo it is often hard to be caught off guard by this type of tenant as long as you do your homework. This means you are going to want to pay close attention to the applicant's credit score, as well as their residency history. If they have been evicted before, this is plenty of reason not to rent to them, especially if you want your first rental property experience to be a smooth one.

The tenant that loves pets: While there is no reason that a person with a pet or two can't make a perfectly outstanding tenant. However, the truth of the matter is that pets cause messes and a property that has previously been rented to a tenant with pets is often difficult to rent to non-pet owners. As such, it is often going to be in your best interest to include a no pet policy in your contract for your first rental property, just to be safe. Unfortunately, pet loving tenants may break this rule, or bring strays onto the property even if you set a limit to the total number of pets instead.

While it can be difficult to determine just how much a prospective tenant loves animals, the best place to start is by talking to the previous landlord. If the tenant has had problems with animals in the past, there is absolutely no reason not to assume that they are going to have additional similar problems in the future. Again, this may not be enough to automatically disqualify a tenant, depending on their past offenses so you will need to keep an eye out for other deal breakers.

Tenants who lie: While not the worst of the worst, assuming they aren't lying about anything major, lying tenants are sure to be nothing but a headache for the entire time they are living in your property. You can expect them to lie about the state of the property when they move in, as well as out, and also do everything they can think of to take advantage of you in hopes of getting extra benefits or discounts.

Unfortunately, it can be difficult to tell a liar from a viable applicant, as you will have very little detail to go off of. As such, it is important that you pay as close attention to the details they do provide you with for signs of deception. While everyone makes mistakes, you are going to want to keep an eye out for indications that the applicant is blatantly lying because if they are already doing so at this stage of your relationship it is unlikely you can expect things to get any better soon.

The tenant who parties too hard: While the definition of partying too hard is going to vary from property to property, it is important that you don't let someone into your property that is going to disrupt the flow of the area by partying too hard. Partying can lead to drunk and disorderly situations, fighting and more; and that's only if they are using legal party favors.

Luckily, assuming you aren't opposed to any and all types of fun taking place in your property, it should be fairly easy to determine if a tenant is going to be a good fit for the culture of the neighborhood. Checking with their references and previous landlord is always a good place to start and a criminal background check should tell you if they like to take their partying to the felonious level.

The tenant who loves drama: While most renters are happy to find a place to live and then fly under the radar until their lease is up, some renters will only be happy if they are constantly dealing with one type of drama or another. This could take the form of constantly asking you for updates on previously agreed upon plans or constantly making mountains out of molehills. Whatever their excuse, you will quickly grow to hate the sound of their voice, guaranteed.

When it comes to pinpointing a dramatic applicant, it can be difficult at first but will get easier with practice. You may notice that they seem a little too enthusiastic throughout the walkthrough and may even eagerly point out small issues that they seem eager to overinflate. They could be curious about the neighbors and see threats when there are none.

A tenant who wants the world: While most tenants understand the give and take that goes into a good landlord/tenant relationship, there are some tenants that feel because they are paying you rent, you are entitled to do everything in your power to make them happy. These sorts of tenants will make your life miserable for the entire length of their say in your property, and feel it is their right to do so.

Luckily, you can easily weed these people out during the interview process as they will be the ones that start complaining about the property right from the start. These won't be valid criticisms either, they will be small issues that the average renter will gladly overlook without a second thought.

A tenant with an eviction on their record: Sure, sometimes bad things happen to good people, but when it comes to your first rental property, taking a risk on a tenant for any reason is never recommended. Luckily, it is easy to weed out the people who you cannot afford to trust at the moment as long as you run a check on their rental history and always do your due diligence before letting anyone put down a deposit.

Tenants who know too much: While you may have a hard time finding a reason to do so, you are going to want to avoid renting out your property to those who are too familiar with the law if at all possible. Lawyers, paralegals and the like are in a position to know every inch of the law and how to exploit it for personal gain. While there is no guarantee this could happen to you, when it comes to your first rental it is better to be safe than sorry.

CONCLUSION

Thank you for making it through to the end of *Rental Property Investing: How to invest in rental properties - The keys to success*, let's hope it was informative and able to provide you with all of the tools you need to achieve your goals, whatever it is that they may be. Just because you've finished this book doesn't mean there is nothing left to learn on the topic, expanding your horizons is the only way to find the mastery you seek. It is important to keep in mind that the real estate market is ever changing, which means that you need to get in the habit of being a lifelong learner if you really hope to find success in the long-term.

Now that you mind is full of ideas regarding your future rental investment property, it can be easy to want to go out and start looking at properties ASAP. It is important to curtail this impulse, however, as there is plenty of research you need to do before you ever set foot in a property that is for sale. Likewise, it is important to have measured expectations when going into the process, don't forget, while a rental property is a viable long-term investment opportunity, if you are making even a thousand dollars a month, on top of paying for a property management company and paying the mortgage, then you are still coming out ahead. Rental property investing can lead to serious wealth, but it won't happen overnight, it is best to think of it as a marathon, not a sprint, slow and steady wins the race.

Finally, if you found this book useful in any way, a review on Amazon is always appreciated!

www.ingramcontent.com/pod-product-compliance
Lightning Source LLC
Chambersburg PA
CBHW052338220526
45472CB00001B/483